Winter's Haiku Symphony
A Seasonal Trilogy

Andy Hoffman

Copyright © 2023 Andy Hoffman
All rights reserved.
ISBN: 9798867492151

Dedicated to the guiding light and enduring warmth of my mother, whose love has been a constant flame through the coldest of winters. These haikus are a testament to the beauty and tranquility that your nurturing spirit has brought into my life. May these verses serve as a source of comfort and solace on the chilly winter nights, wrapping you in the same love and coziness you've selflessly shared with me. In each haiku, find a reflection of the warmth you've instilled in my heart. With love and gratitude, these words are offered to you, my dearest mother, as a reminder of the enduring light you bring to every season of my life.

Imagine yourself cozied up by the fireside, a steaming mug of cocoa cradled in your hands, as you embark on a delightful journey through these haikus. Each verse is crafted to be sipped slowly, like the comforting warmth of a winter beverage. Take your time with these poetic sips, letting the words cascade gently over your senses. Much like the gradual warmth spreading through your body with each sip, these haikus invite you to savor the imagery and emotion, one carefully composed phrase at a time. Let the winter scenes unfold leisurely in your mind, and relish the beauty of the season in small, unhurried sips. These verses are meant to be a literary indulgence, offering a taste of the serene and enchanting moments that winter brings, savored slowly for a richer experience.

Part One
Early Winter

Frost-kissed daisies weep,
Winter's breath in silent morn,
Nature's lullaby.

Icy tendrils grasp,
Leaves surrender to the cold,
Autumn's final sigh.

Snowflakes dance and twirl,
   Blanket of serenity,
  Winter's soft embrace.

Solitude descends,
Bare branches whisper secrets,
Snowflakes keep them hushed.

Crystal mornings gleam,
Sunlight glistens on the snow,
Nature's diamond coat.

Gray skies hold their tears,
Frozen teardrops on the earth,
Winter's silent grief.

Footprints in the snow,
Memories etched in each step,
Winter's diary.

Shadows in the dusk,
Bare trees reach for the twilight,
Chilly silent eve.

Cold winds weave a tale,
Nature's breath in frozen air,
Winter's whispered song.

Winter's breath is crisp,
Silence wrapped in frosty air,
Nature's quiet hymn.

Geese in formation,
Honking through the wintry sky,
Farewell to the warmth.

Icicles hanging,
Nature's fragile artwork,
Frozen masterpiece.

Frozen lakes shimmer,
Reflecting the pale sunlight,
Winter's glassy gaze.

Chimney's gentle smoke,
Curling in the frigid air,
Winter's warm exhale.

Hibernating world,
Dreams beneath the snowy quilt,
Silent peaceful rest.

Naked trees stand tall,
Resolute in frozen grasp,
Nature's stoic pose.

Frost on windowpanes,
Nature's delicate lacework,
Icy intricate art.

Sunsets painted gold,
Winter's canvas illuminated,
Nature's fiery brush.

Shadows in the snow,
Whispers of a silent world,
Winter's secret tale.

Evening moonlight casts,
Silver glow on sleeping earth,
Nature's tranquil night.

Evergreen sentinels,
Guarding against icy chill,
Nature's steadfast watch.

Snow-covered rooftops,
Blanketed in quiet white,
Frozen peaceful hush.

Frozen breath hangs still,
A misty waltz in the air,
Nature's chilly dance.

Winter stars emerge,
Night's diamonds in the cold sky,
Nature's celestial display.

Morning frost retreats,
Sunlight melts the icy hold,
Modest gentle thaw.

Silent snowfall drifts,
Nature's whispered lullaby,
Winter's soft caress.

Crisp air bites the cheeks,
Footprints mark the snowy path,
Nature's wintry tale.

Winter's palette fades,
Grayscale landscape, tranquil hush,
Nature's muted scene.

Pines cloaked in snowfall,
Stoic guardians of the woods,
Winter's silent keepers.

Early winter's breath,
Nature sighs in frozen air,
A season's quiet close.

Part Two
Midwinter

Frozen river's breath,
Crystals in the icy flow,
Frigid silent stream.

Snowflakes softly fall,
Blanketing the world in white,
Icy gentle touch.

Ice-kissed windowpanes,
Nature's arctic artwork,
Frigid fractal forms.

Shadows on the snow,
Whispered tales of ancient pines,
Solstice solemn song.

Hushed footsteps on ice,
Echoes in the frozen air,
Winter's quiet path.

Frosty breath suspended,
Crystal exhale in the chill,
Wintry icy sigh.

Twilight's early blush,
Daylight's fleeting visit ends,
Night grows longer still.

Frozen moon hangs low,
Silver orb in midnight sky,
Nature's cosmic watch.

Icicles dangling,
Nature's glassy chandeliers,
Cold delicate art.

Snow-laden branches,
A weighty burden of white,
Evergreens kowtow.

Earth sleeps beneath snow,
Dreams in a cold, silent slumber,
Winter's deep repose.

Silent owl on watch,
Feathers cloaked in wintry hues,
Nature's sentinel.

Frozen ponds reflect,
Winter's stillness in the ice,
Nature's mirrored calm.

Snowflakes twirl and spin,
A delicate ballet dance,
Frigid frozen waltz.

Crisp air bites the skin,
Nature's sharp, invigorating,
Winter's bracing breath.

Footprints in the snow,
Trails of stories left behind,
Winter's narrative.

Frost on evergreens,
Nature's icy decoration,
Winter's adornment.

Silence in the woods,
Bare trees stand in contemplation,
Winter's meditation.

Gray clouds overhead,
Snowflakes weave a soft curtain,
Nature's quiet veil.

Sleet taps on windows,
Winter's percussive lullaby,
Nature's rhythmic beat.

Chimney smoke rises,
Cozy hearths in frozen nights,
Winter's warm respite.

Aurora shimmers,
Winter's dance of colored lights,
Nature's celestial show.

Hibernating world,
Life beneath the snowy quilt,
Winter's dormant peace.

Starlight on the snow,
Diamonds in the frozen night,
Winter's cosmic glow.

Frozen pond's stillness,
Reflections in icy glass,
Nature's tranquil mirror.

Crystalline hoarfrost,
Glistening on every branch,
Winter's diamond dust.

Winter winds whisper,
Secrets in the frosted air,
Nature's soft confide.

Moonlit snowscape gleams,
Silver threads in the night sky,
Winter's ethereal dream.

Pine trees in repose,
Cloaked in snowy stillness,
Winter's silent guard.

Cold embraces all,
Nature's frosty symphony,
Winter's frozen hymn.

Part Three
Late Winter

Winter's waning breath,
Melting snow reveals the earth,
Nature stirs awake.

Distant robins sing,
A herald of warmer days,
Winter's fading song.

Buds on sleeping trees,
Promise of rebirth to come,
Nature's silent hope.

Frosty mornings fade,
Sunlight lingers a bit more,
Late winter's soft glow.

Icicles drip down,
Tears of winter's parting sigh,
Nature's slow goodbye.

Thawing river's flow,
A liquid dance to freedom,
Winter's chains released.

Flowers pierce the snow,
Delicate blooms in the cold,
Nature's early bloom.

Winter's grip gives way,
Emerging crocus whispers,
Nature's silent bloom.

Daffodils stand tall,
Golden trumpets herald spring,
Winter's final bow.

Days grow longer now,
Winter's shadow softly fades,
Nature's lengthening.

Chirping sparrows play,
Melodies in warming air,
Late winter's encore.

Melted snow reveals,
Fragile buds on sleeping twigs,
Nature's silent birth.

Frost-kissed petals bloom,
Crocuses open wide,
Winter's tender kiss.

Trees stretch in the sun,
Buds unfurling in the warmth,
Nature's slow embrace.

Warmer winds whisper,
Snowflakes turn to droplets bright,
Late winter's soft thaw.

Sunlit icicles,
Glistening in the noonday,
Winter's final gleam.

Robins on the lawn,
Signs of spring in their chatter,
Nature's joyful tune.

Snowmen fade away,
Carrot noses in the mud,
Winter's slow retreat.

Crisp air turns milder,
Winter's chill begins to fade,
Nature's warming hug.

Thawing earth exhales,
Scent of rebirth in the air,
Nature's fragrant sigh.

Snowbanks recede,
Revealing patches of green,
Winter's end in sight.

Winter's final frost,
Petals tinged with morning chill,
Nature's fragile bloom.

Crocuses peek out,
Purple and gold in the thaw,
Late winter's debut.

Sunsets painted warm,
Winter's palette turns to spring,
Nature's vibrant hues.

Geese in formation,
Heading north with purpose,
Winter's farewell flight.

Ice patches shimmer,
Sunlight dancing on the thaw,
Nature's liquid grace.

Snowflakes turn to rain,
Gentle drops on winter's stage,
Late winter's encore.

Warmth in every breeze,
Winter yields to gentle spring,
Nature's soft caress.

Cherry blossoms bloom,
Winter's memory fades fast,
Nature's grand encore.

Made in United States
Orlando, FL
27 November 2023